Who You Grow Into

poems by

Amy Le Ann Richardson

Finishing Line Press
Georgetown, Kentucky

Who You Grow Into

ACKNOWLEDGMENTS

These poems began during the Covid Garden Workshop in 2020 led by
Rebecca Gayle Howell and made possible by Appalshop and the National
Endowment for the Arts. They were crafted from prose written as an
exercise based on Ross Gay's *Book of Delights*, asking us to focus on a small
moment of delight we experienced each day. I wrote many of these vignettes
exploring the nooks and crannies of my life on the farm and my connection
to the land and my family. Writing them transformed me, shifting my
focus from the panic of the pandemic that autumn onto gratitude and onto
all of the small reasons life continued to be amazing despite the tragedy
surrounding me.

I collected them in a document, and once the workshop ended, I gradually
stopped writing them. They sat untouched on my computer for a year
before I read through them again, rediscovering my delight and selecting a
few, pulling out details, and crafting them into poems during the 2021 Fall
Writers Retreat at Hindman Settlement School.

Publisher: Leah Huete de Maines
Editor: Christen Kincaid
Cover Art: Thelia River Richardson
Author Photo: Tina Brouwer
Cover Design: Elizabeth Maines McCleavy

Order online: www.finishinglinepress.com
also available on amazon.com

Author inquiries and mail orders:
Finishing Line Press
PO Box 1626
Georgetown, Kentucky 40324
USA

Contents

For my family.
May we continue to weave a legacy of stories into the soil

Post-Harvest

First frost feels like the end,
but it's the beginning
of thinking about next year,
preparing for sugaring season,
transitioning.
I walk through the gardens after harvest,
rummaging what's left on dying vines and
dried out stems, touching their crisp shells
one last time
remembering working in the rows
while kids crawled to weed tender baby plants.
Standing among scattered corn husks,
reflecting on my breakdown as the stalks
rustled in the breeze back in August.

Thinking about what I'll do different next season
as I collect seeds from mature okra pods and milkweeds
scavenging the few ground cherries left
scattered in among the weeds and corn fodder
we cut down a few days ago.
Holding the potential for the future in my hands
feels powerful, and the crisp air brushing against my skin
makes me feel alive.

The sun warms my face as I work,
inhaling deep breaths of cut hay and morning glories,
smelling my fingers between picking because
it may be the last time my hands smell like tomato vines
until next spring when I'm setting out new plants.
The ones I work my way through,
plucking off the last green tomatoes that
survived the frost last night are done and
now it's time to rip them out.
Most everything in this garden was
picked and eaten or preserved,
our summer garden is finished.

Recollections

This morning I walked to the
chicken coop to collect eggs.
The crisp air drew me outside.

I walked past raspberry briars and
apple tree grafts healing and growing
along the road.

I walked with the frost-tipped grass
crunching under my boots,
swinging the egg basket in my hand
like a kid, almost skipping.

Giddy.

There's something about being cold outside,
then walking back into your warm house,
about the way hot coffee tastes
better on frosty mornings.

I remember dare games with my neighbors as a kid
we'd see who could hold their hands longest in
the freezing creek water running along our yards.

We'd play outside until our lips were blue and
we could barely move our fingers, then run
back to our houses and have one of our moms
make hot chocolate, and if we were lucky
she'd give us cookies too.

I always loved how it felt as my body warmed back up.

It made me feel alive. It still does.
I love waking early and wandering out on
cold mornings just to feel it again,
like I did when I was a kid.

With the warm chicken eggs in my basket,
I know going back inside is going to bring
piping hot coffee and a fresh breakfast that
warms me from the inside out

just like the hot chocolate in my memory.

Rainy days mean chili.

Channing got a deer over the weekend,
so today it's chili as fresh as it gets with our own
butternut squash and herbs and onions all mixed in.

The house smells delicious

it's aroma seeping through the walls into every space,
the cornbread in the oven warming it like my
grandma's house always was because

she was always cooking something.

Now, I use her cast iron skillet for
cornbread and biscuits and cobblers,
she's still passing on her love through my food.

It feels alive in here.

All this food grown and processed and
made by our hands. It tastes better like our taste buds know
about the hands that worked

to plant those seeds,
pick that squash,
skin that deer and grind the meat,
pick those herbs and dry them
hanging on the board over the kitchen sink.

Turns the Mood

I was in a bad mood.
Running on little sleep,
knots of anxiety hanging in my belly.
I knew my kids' moods would
reflect my own.

We were a grumpy mess
at the dining table with coffee and
books and to-do lists spread out,
rain hitting the roof, each waiting for
someone else to make the first move.

Usually, we were distracted with gardens,
but that's all winding down, and we're in a lull before
we bust it out to tap trees for sugaring.

It was dark earlier and they were inside more.
The rain kept pouring, and I'd had enough.
In sudden inspiration, I declared,
"We're playing in the rain!"

Both kids stared like I had lost my mind.
The oldest protested. However, once they were out with
the warm rain bouncing off their jackets
and the ground squishing beneath muck boots,
everyone was on board.

We set off up the holler with the dog running wild circles around us.

Sang songs, "Pitter patter pitter patter listen to the rain,"
as we splashed streams and puddles sending
brightly colored leaves in all directions.
Waded up the creek and watched the
fog descend around us like a falling cloud.

We found turtles and purple jelly fungus.

Being in the woods, remembering how good it feels to stand outside soaking wet changed the course of the day.

Acorn Bread

Today, the weather made everything okay for a little while.
Sunshine soaking into my skin always puts me in a better mood,
and watching my kids play outside just being kids is the best feeling
amid uncertainty and chaos.

I know they worry.

We have discussions about science and beliefs and
the election often enough for me to know
how heavily it weighs on them.
I have more faith in their generation than I do my own.
Their resilience and adaptability amaze me.

Their empathy, their willingness to learn and to do better—
it gives me hope.
They remind me of my garden.
Seeds I've planted with nothing more to go on
than hope and faith that the weather will hold,
pests won't invade,
that I did everything I was supposed to help them grow.

And it is hard, but so sweet.

This morning, we gathered eggs together
walking through remains of our garden,
collecting lingering raspberries, taking in those last tart treats and
discussing our plans.
Thelia swung the egg basket and
Bryum alternated galloping and walking.
We decided to collect acorns to make flour, so
we took off to the woods.

It's the place that puts us in a better mood
whether it's the way the sunlight
filters through the trees, the delicious mushrooms we forage, or just
sitting in the shade beneath an oak tree delighting in the acorns,
especially the ones with hats.

It's the reason we focus on agroforestry and
sustainable agriculture at our farm.

We want this to be here for future generations, so we feel like what we
choose to do, and what we teach our kids
about farming and the woods is the most
important thing we are doing.
It all fits together. We need the land, and
there is so much to be grateful for.

Picking up acorns with my kids was my favorite part of today.

Our dog, Whiskey, ran around rooting through the leaves,
eating a few acorns herself.
We stuffed them into tote bags as we discussed how
Native people here made acorn four.
We planned a meal and what other fall goodies
we could forage to have too.

They worked all evening peeling acorns and preparing them to make
meal while I cooked dinner.
I can't wait until it's ready to eat.

Homegrown

Channing and the kids roasted beets and potatoes
with smoked sausage and sautéed kale.
The smell filled me up from the doorway,
and I ate until I was stuffed.

We dug those potatoes a few days ago,
Thelia and I racing to see who could
grab the bigger ones first as
Channing and Bryum took turns
loosening the mounds of dirt with the shovel.

The kids pulled the beets this morning and picked kale,
venturing out in the cold, misty air just for the occasion.

I don't know if it was because I was hungry
or if it was memories tied to each piece of our meal
or maybe because our family cooked together,

but it was the finest food,

the potatoes and beets perfectly crispy on the outside,
the kale just salty enough, and sausage
bursting with flavor.

Flames

I lit a candle today because
I just couldn't feel warm.
It isn't cold in my house,
but I don't hold onto heat.

I'm always cold.

My candle makes the room feel warmer,
even though one isn't enough to
produce any real heat.

Something about the glow of candlelight
soaks into your skin and your eyes, especially
if the only light is the flickering flame
casting shadows across the walls.

It takes me back to campfires,

the warm glow pressed against my legs,
cool dew falling around the edges just
beyond the heat of the firelight,

hot summer nights telling stories
roasting marshmallows
staying up well past bedtime.

The thin line of smoke rising from the
flame small, but pulling forth moments
smoke invaded my nostrils,
chasing me around the fire ring in
attempt to escape, but always landing
right in my face no matter where I sat.

Maybe memories are what warm me.

Pressed into the glow of the candle,
I can feel the heat of summer.

Warmed Three Times

I move wood this time of year.
We all do.
Channing fells dead trees or
finds ones that have fallen
and cuts them into thick slices.

The kids and I load them,
haul them to the front yard,
split them into smaller pieces that
will fit into our stove, and then
put them in neat stacks.

It's tedious work, but important.

Pick up.
Stack.
Repeat.

Knowing on freezing days
we will have enough wood to
keep our home warm.
Knowing when we're boiling sap
we'll have enough to run the evaporator
and make syrup, thick steam rising to the ceiling.

I find Bess bugs and wooly worms
hidden in decaying bark as
I move piece upon piece into the greenhouse
that was filled with tender young plants this spring,
but is now halfway full of firewood.

I pause to consider the cycles playing out
right here in our greenhouse,
a place most only think of as the beginning,
the place we start seeds,
but farming doesn't allow for spaces that

serve only one purpose.

Take Only Pictures

Gray clouds loom overhead
I taste rain in the air.
Even the birds are quiet.
Mornings like this are
somber,
reflective.
I walk through the woods
searching for mushrooms.
The deep instinctual urge to prepare,
gather resources and hunker down
overcomes me this time of year.
The heavy smell of a coming
rainstorm only intensifies it.
I've felt this way since the
beginning of covid on some level—
hunker down,
prepare,
stay alert—
deep animal instincts when
danger sits on the horizon.
Too many people seem to have
lost touch with that part of themselves,
and I wonder if it's because we've
moved so far from the earth,
but we are no more above the frailties and
dangers of nature than the chipmunk who
darts across my path screeching a
warning call out to his friends.
Maybe we are more susceptible due to
our rejection of our place amid natural cycles and
our rejection of the impact we've had on them,
how they've changed
because of our wants.

I crunch through fallen leaves,
stepping over long roots,
tripping on the occasional rock.
I think back to conversations
about taking only what we need,
composting and giving back
nutrients to the soil,
how the forest does this all on its own.

Seasonal Shifts

I cleaned the kitchen today.
Took apart the stove
scrubbed down the cabinets.
Wiped all surfaces with blue dawn and bleach.

I do this when the weather turns in fall.

We're done with preserving this year.
No more dehydrating tomatoes and shiitakes or
pressure canning beans and tomato juice and bone broth
or strawberry, blackberry or pawpaw jams and jellies.

We may have a few days of canning venison
coming in November, but it's not the
constant busy kitchen we keep in summer.
Some days, I miss the hum of the dehydrator
or the hiss of the pressure canner.

The sweet sticky smell of jam and the open
screen doors wafting in honeysuckle and heat.

Constantly washing jars and picking veggies,
and hoeing weeds, and spending those long days
outside until lightning bugs rose from the
creek banks to greet us.

My bare feet moving from lush grass
to tilled earth
to warm kitchen linoleum,
I know it will come again next year.

Now, it's time for soups and opening the jars I watched
my kids' small hands pack with beans or ladle juice into.
It's time to shift gears, cut firewood, sow cover crops, and
prepare to tap trees.

Soon it will be time to sit in the sugar shack with steam that smells like pancakes surrounding me as I read novels and stoke the fire in the evaporator,

browse seed catalogs,
and think about spring.

Preservation

We're building an off-grid cabin.
We need to get away from screens and phones
and the constant barrage of information.
We need to finish digging potatoes.
The only road here is gravel and
it's steep enough that you'd have to
know where you're heading to drive up it.
It's quiet.
I love it.
The sun is hazy giving it an ethereal glow
it typically only has when it's snowing,
but it the air is warm and the edges of the forest
hold tightly to crisp leaves and bold autumn colors,
and the scent of sweet hay lingers in the breeze.
There is a foreboding transition
spread across the landscape crying out to me to
pay attention
these moments matter most.
I think of the many times
I've had to leave people and places
I still hold reverence for within me.
I think of holding my children through
their first harsh realizations that
nothing lasts forever,
and people we love die
explaining how many feelings can all
swirl inside you at the same time like a whirlpool
how you can love and be happy for memories,

but sad and angry there will be no more
how you can grieve and cherish and hold
space for all those feelings
how it never goes away,
but eventually fits as a piece of
who you grow into.
I'm living a transition now, but it is different than
moving to a new place or losing a loved one.

It's hard to name.
It stretches out across the months like the hazy winter sun
kissing those autumn brushed fields in summer temperatures,
everything is out of place and life has taken on a new context.
I hope it pushes me to grow around the
pain of existing in these times to be stronger.
To evolve and to hold this time as a piece of who I become.

Sweet Cookie Memory

I made maple black walnut
cookies for breakfast this morning.
Three years ago, I wrote this recipe
after months of tinkering.

Trying varying amounts of ingredients and
enlisting my family as taste-testers.

By the time I perfected it,
we'd all had enough maple cookies
for a while, but I got it the way I wanted—
soft, chewy, and sweet but not too sweet,
holding the flavor of our syrup enough to
mingle well with the black walnuts.

I made these cookies to sell at the
farmers' market and other events.
I hadn't made them since last winter,
and I had to look back at my recipe.

The first time I took them to an event,
it was the Kentucky Proud Expo.
At first, we weren't selling many
compared to our other products,
but then a lady who had bought
one package that morning came back.

She said she wanted every cookie I had
and bought them all.

She told us they tasted like cookies
her grandmother made, and she hadn't
had any like that since she had passed
away a few years ago.

It was one of my favorite moments
in our years of selling food.

Imprinted Here

I walked today.
I like to take inventory of
the woods along the trail.
There are several box turtles
we frequently see,
often in the same places
along our path,
but none this time.
I know each tree lining the way,
the big rocks and cliff lines,
the way the breeze swirls and
shakes tree limbs in the
canopy above me.
I loved watching changes as
the greenery transformed to
a rainbow of colors and
leaves slicked the ground
crunching too loudly
for any kind of stealth.
Sometimes, by the old
smokehouse still standing
where the original home on
the land is now no more than
a pile of old bricks from the
brickyard that used to be
over in town, I can stand still
and feel the history of this place
surrounding me.
It makes me shudder
when I am alone.
Not from fear, but in the way
something bigger than yourself
makes you pause to take it all in.
Goosebumps.
I don't know all the stories yet,

but in the tranquility of late evening,
these hollows bleed the story
of the woods into my brain.

Memories Layered Like Stack Cake

Growing up, I spent most
weekends with my grandma.
I was her only grandchild and
she always made me feel like
I was the most important person.
She taught me how to sew
and embroider and make biscuits,
and we spent a lot of time
piddling in her wood shop.
She loved to make things.
She could make anything.
I found a turtle shell once, and
I was upset the turtle had died,
so she took it and made a stuffed
turtle that fit into the shell, and
fashioned it to look like a
real one just for me.
She often made me necklaces
shaped like animals cut from thin
pieces of wood and painted and
she tied on all different kinds of ribbon.

She always cooked for us on Sundays
her food was the best.
Gravy and biscuits,
chicken and dumplings,
beef stew and cornbread,
and she baked the best cakes.
I inherited the Pyrex bowl she
mixed batter in and her cast iron skillet.
I use them every day, and I feel her
with me in the kitchen.

I often wonder about Channing's
grandmother too.
I never met her, but
my kitchen was her kitchen.

She must have cooked hundreds of meals here,
and there is something profound about
sharing a kitchen, even if the
time frame doesn't overlap.

Unearth Magic

We saw a red spotted newt
today up at the head of our holler
by the cave where the trail we built
curves and turns to go up along cliffs
at the top of the ridge.

It was right there where the ascent
begins and the cave comes into view.
It stood out, it's stark orange a contrast
to all the now brown leaves
scattered around the forest floor.

We all stopped to admire it.

Watching it slowly extend its little
legs and crawl across the big
sycamore and pawpaw leaves.

I took a short video at the
insistence of the kids,
so we could remember it,
and watch it repeatedly
to admire its beauty and
its existence here in our woods.

Childhood fades so quickly,
I hope some of this magic
stays with them into their adult
lives as they grow and the world
tries to beat them down.

I hope seeps in their skin
through bare feet and weaves
right into the roots of trees they climb,
I hope they come back and
visit these moments and
remember worrying over the

tiny inhabitants of the forest.

I hope they know how much it matters.

Rendered

It was opening day of deer season.
Channing got one early and brought
it back to the house.

He cut it up out in the yard,
brought it in, and we cut it into
smaller pieces and put it in
quart jars to can.

Our freezer is already full,
and it keeps a long while this way.

It also makes for some quick,
easy dinners when I don't have
time to thaw something out.

Sometimes we put potatoes
and onions or sweet potatoes
and herbs in with it as we stuff it
into jars, so it makes a stew.

On the cold days of winter,
I like opening a jar and mixing

it with cream of mushroom soup
and making a side of biscuits.
It's hardy and filling

such a comfort after
being out in the weather
when we're sugaring.
I love having shelves of our

work stored away in the basement
holding promises for future meals

we'll enjoy as we remember what
went into putting them all up.
It tastes better when you know,

and when you know the hands that
labored to bring it to your table.

Squash Soup

Today, we ate carrots the kids planted.
Cosmic purple. Like a rainbow.
They are beautiful and delicious.
This time of year, everything that
comes from the garden tastes richer.
Maybe it's the frosts making
the root vegetables sweeter.
Maybe it's because
fresh food is growing scarcer.
Whatever it is, those carrots
exploded with flavor,
and made me even gladder for
the beauty soil gives us.
I made soup too with butternut
squash we store in the basement.
They keep well and
I am always glad to have them.
I don't like colder weather,
but this year I am relishing these days
and the warmth of soups and fires.
There is something about the
sensation of cold seeping
deep into your skin, and then
walking into a warm house.
It reminds me how
much I have
to be grateful for.

Additional Acknowledgments

A huge thanks to Rebecca Gayle Howell for planting the seed that inspired these poems as well as reminding me my story matters and encouraging me to release it into the world. Thanks to Hindman Settlement School for being a sanctuary for writers and to the inspiring, supportive community who exist there. Hindman is truly more than a place, and I am filled with gratitude to be part of it. Thanks also to Melissa Helton for reading my manuscript and being a dear friend to me in so many ways.

I am grateful, as well, to the Kentucky Foundation for Women for grant and residency opportunities that have allowed me time, space, and funding to work on parts of several projects, including this chapbook. Without resources they have provided, this wouldn't have been possible, and I have immense gratitude for them, their mission, and their continual effort to highlight feminist voices throughout Kentucky.

Thanks, of course, to my family who not only tolerate my eccentric habits, but also allow me time and space with endearment and understanding. Nothing is more motivating than my children's enthusiasm to read my work, and nothing helps me do the work like knowing they are cared for while I disappear to retreats and workshops—thanks to my generous life partner, Channing, and my parents who not only help us care for our children, but also often foot the bill when we cannot. I was fortunate they raised me surrounded by love and nature and never having to question their support. Thanks to my children, Bryum and Thelia, for teaching me again and again what life is and for always reminding me to pause. And, as I'm sure is obvious upon reading this collection, none of these poems would exist without these people with whom I share a life. A life I treasure. I am truly privileged.

Thanks to my encouragers and supporters who continue to shine light into my days in numerous ways. I am grateful to exist within a community of such love and pure intentions toward our fellow humans and our environment. I owe so many pieces of who I am to more people than I can count in these pages, and I hold you all with deep affection.

Amy Le Ann Richardson was born and raised in Morehead, KY. She grew up running through the hills with cousins and walking barefoot through her parents' garden letting her imagination run wild. Her love of stories led her to earn her Bachelor's in English from Morehead State University ('07) and MFA in Writing from Spalding University ('09). She moved to Oklahoma for five years after completing her MFA where she became a mother and decided Kentucky is where she belongs. So, she moved back home and she and her husband, Channing, worked to turn his family land from an old tobacco farm into a small-scale sustainable farm they named Forgotten Foods Farm. Amy has taught and worked as an academic advisor at Morehead State University, and is actively involved with Red Oaks Forest School, a nonprofit centered on reconnecting children and families with nature.

Amy is a writer and visual artist deeply concerned with environmental issues and her work has been featured in *Black Moon Magazine, Pine Mountain Sand & Gravel, The Yearling,* and *Kentucky Monthly*. She has received grants and fellowships from the Kentucky Foundation for Women and her visual art show, *The Curiosity Cabinet Collection*, featuring 29 wood-burning and acrylic mixed media pieces on reclaimed cabinet doors and 30 original poems was displayed at the Rowan County Arts Center from December 2022 to February 2023. Amy lives and works on her family farm in Carter County, Kentucky writing poems and stories, growing veggies, making maple syrup, and homeschooling her kids with her husband, Channing. Learn more and follow her adventures at *www.amyleannrichardson.com*

www.ingramcontent.com/pod-product-compliance
Lightning Source LLC
Chambersburg PA
CBHW022055080426
42734CB00009B/1350